WHAT THEY'RE SAYING ABOUT
LIFE'S FUNNIEST STORIES

"Nice job, honey...I'm not in there am I?"

— Kristin Oberts (my lovely wife)

"Did anybody pay you to do this? If not, they're getting what its worth."

— A.J. Oberts (my supportive father)

"You did what with my picture!!"

— Annalise Oberts (my independent daughter)

"Heh, heh...cool."

— Kellen Oberts (my artistic son)

"It did too happen that way!"

— Mallory Oberts (my care-giving daughter-in-law)

"That's my boy."

— M. Oberts (this is what my mother would've said a few years ago)

"Hey Gar, ya done pulled together a good'un, but I don't git it?!"

— Virgil (see later text on this genius)

"God has ways of ...oops, gotta go."

— Monsignor Gas

"If I could, I would buy a million copies of this book!"

— Harry Roberts (ah, just a guy I know who reads books)

LIFE'S FUNNIEST STORIES

*A Collection of Life's Laugh-Out-Loud Stories
from Friends, Family and Self*

Oberts Books
Tustin, CA
www.lifesfunnieststories.com

By Gary L. Oberts
All Rights Reserved © 2011 Gary L. Oberts

Published by Gary L. Oberts
Oberts Books
Printed in the United States of America

Author: Gary L. Oberts
Graphic Design: Kellen Oberts

13-digit ISBN: 978-0-6154523-4-0
10-digit ISBN: 0-6154523-4-5

First Printing

PREFACE

Have you ever been lying in bed, unable to sleep and remembered a story from your past that caused you to break out in laughter? The more you try to stifle it so you don't wake your mate, the more the bed shakes. How about in church? Remember Mary Tyler Moore and the clown funeral? Well, it's those stories that I tried to collect and put into this book. I have a few of my own, but I needed more so I sent out a request to family and friends that I knew had a good sense of humor. My hope is that you find them as entertaining as I do.

You will notice as you work your way through this book, that many of the stories pertain to stupid things that people do sometimes... Lord knows there's a great supply of that to go around. But nothing gets a good laugh as quickly as potty humor. Take for example that cover picture of my son sitting on a rental horse waiting for his ride to begin. It was just a matter of good timing that I had a camera in my hand at the time. My apologies in advance if you are offended by such things...maybe it would be better that you put the book down now before you get too far.

Every one of the stories is absolutely true, so please don't be too offended if some of them make you blush. Just have a chuckle and move on. Enjoy! G.L.O.

THANKS

My thanks go out to all of the people who volunteered their funniest stories for me to share with you. I was maybe too selective in sorting through all of those submitted, but whether in this collection or not, I thank you. Special thanks to Kellen for his graphic layout and editing help, and of course, for being on that horse at that special time.

A GOOD SOURCE OF INCOME

I went to my dentist one day with a tooth problem. She sent me to an endodontics specialist. Neither one of them could determine what my problem was, but both charged me for the analysis. If I got paid for everything I don't know, I'd be a billionaire.

Author

TOODSIE'S FIRST BIG GIRL PEE

Our daughter A. (name withheld to avoid embarrassment) was typical of little girls growing up with a big brother – she wanted to imitate everything she saw her brother do. So we were not surprised when at about two-years old she announced to us that she was ready to go potty "just like big brother".

So we all marched into the bathroom – big brother included – to watch our little girl with her first big girl pee. She proceeded to walk up to the toilet – just like big brother, drop her drawers – just like big brother, and stand there – just like just like big brother - peeing all over herself, the floor, the three of us, plus the cat who had wandered in out of curiosity. She stood erect, just like big brother, and squirted everything in site. It was so funny and unexpected that all we could do for a few seconds was laugh, before my wife yelled "No, like mommy!" but it was too late.

Author

IN THE BOYS ROOM

One day during junior high school, I walked into the boys' bathroom, and was greeted by Bill, a friend of mine. Bill stuttered terribly. Possibly because of his speech impediment, he desperately wanted to be cool. Spotting me, his face lit up, he reached into his pocket, and pulled out a switchblade knife that he had somehow just acquired.

As he flipped the blade open, he cried out "Hey nnn..., nnn..., nnn..., nnn...Dave, nnn..., nnn..., nnn..., nnn..., nnn... think fast!"

Dave B., St. Paul, MN

WHAT?!

A friend of mine, Arnie, and I were driving down toward San Diego with our wives, with the radio tuned into news and traffic reports. A report of a serious automobile accident came on, and, after the reporter stopped talking, Arnie and I glanced at each other, and he said "did you just hear what I thought I heard?" Yes, we both heard the announcer describe the accident as one in which "....three people were killed, two of them seriously!" ....We never did hear how the third one made out!

Larry W., CA

DID I HEAR THAT CORRECTLY, HONEY

The five-year old is strapped in the backseat.

We parents are strapped in front.

A temporary silence is shattered by our daughter's exclamation of "F*#@ing Succotash!" and her clapping with glee.

I hear my wife's neck vertebrae snap as she wheels her head to glare at me. I am speechless--I don't know whether to defend myself or go with my first instinct to laugh--when the kid lets it rip again!

Laughing is definitely not the way to go now, so I ask our little sweetheart what she was trying to say.

"F*#@ing Succotash!" is her reply. Damn (I thought).

My wife then asks in a very measured tone, "Were you trying to say *sufferin' succotash* like the cartoons?"

"Yes Mummy," came the reply I was hoping for; followed by... "f*#@ng succotash."

Steve W., St. Paul, MN

THE INCOMPREHENSIBILITY RUB

Our corner neighborhood drug store in Pittsburgh served a large population of European transplants. The pharmacist was their doctor for any number of ailments, from clearing particles of soot out of the eye to giving family advice, most of which I had no training for. But that didn't matter...I was free. I was even asked once to fit a diaphragm.

Hardly a week would go by when a customer would not come in apprehensive over the nature of their "BMs" (bowel movements). They would ask me why it used to be soft and now it's hard, or used to be fat now it's thin. I would hear that it used to be brown and now it's tan, or it used to be long and now it's short. A not so old customer came in wanting to know why it used to sink and now it floats.

I developed a stylized stance for such disasters. I would tuck my left hand into my right arm pit, thumb on the outside. Place my thumb and pinky finger spread across my forehead, slowly moving back and forth, my head looking down. I call it the "incomprehensibility rub." It was incomprehensible to me that someone would actually give me this kind of information. So I am trying to look thoughtful but actually trying to control my shoulders from bouncing up and down and myself from losing it and bursting into laughter.

Jerry. F., Tustin, CA

CAREFUL WHAT YOU SAY!

My wife and I were coming home from a funeral. She digs me still, so it wasn't entirely surprising to hear her testify that her love for me was such that she would have a very hard time going on without me if I died. She then said, "I hope I die before you do so I wouldn't have to go through that."

Guys, if your spouse ever says this to you, do not reply, "I hope you do, too."

Steve W., St. Paul, MN

FACTORY LIFE

Tommy

I worked in a paint factory to earn money during my high school and college days. This was a real eye-opening experience to a young suburban white kid. The single-most important thing it taught me was that I needed to keep my grades high enough to make sure I didn't have to do this the rest of my life.

Among the groups of people working in this Illinois factory was a contingent of what I would call Kentucky hill folk. This was a hard working group, but they did not have the benefit of much education. They also all seemed to be related somehow.

The youngest member of this group was Tommy. Tommy had about four teeth. I say about because I could never quite focus on how many there were, since those that were there were half black and hard to get a read on. Among my favorite sayings from these guys was "gitchee", as in "You need to gitchee a hammer". But the absolute funniest thing I ever heard was from Tommy. He was asked by the foreman if he had accomplished a certain task, to which he responded "I already done do-ed it".

Virgil

Tommy's cousin, Virgil, also worked with us in the factory. Compared to Virgil, Tommy was the Einstein of the family. Virgil suspiciously "hurt his back" once and managed to wrangle $500 out of the company if he would sign a release never to approach them for money again. He of course did trade away any future recourse to get his hands on that cash. With his new found riches in hand, Virgil headed off to Kentucky on a Friday after work and proceeded to buy $500 in fireworks and shoot them all off during his whirlwind trip. He returned to work on Monday and had to borrow money for lunch.

Another great memory of Virgil's wit was when he whistled at a fellow worker's wife as the two walked by him. The guy who was with his wife, Dave, used to work concrete construction for a living before coming to the paint factory, so he was rather strong. He turned and in one fast movement picked Virgil up by the front of his shirt and lifted him two feet off of the ground slamming him into a stack of paint boxes. He showed remarkable constraint in not doing Virgil a lot of bodily harm – needless to say, Virgil pledged never to get close to Dave or his wife in the future. I'm not sure I heard this clearly, but I think I heard some of the fireworks come out of Virgil's lower regions during this encounter.

Tony
We also had a Polish group of immigrants. Among them was Tony. Some of this group of mixed men and women were fair at English, but Tony was an old guy who just couldn't seem to get it. While checking his shipment one time, I saw that an order headed to Wisconsin was not likely to get to the right spot. Every box that he had stenciled was being sent to "Meevaakie".

Ron
One of the other characters at the factory was Ron, who had an unusual trait. His navel was located at about a 45 degree angle off to the right of where they are normally located. When he stood with his hands on his hips, one hand was on his stomach and the other on his back.

Shipping Clerk
Unfortunately, another of my primary lessons I learned from working in a factory to get through college was to swear like a sailor. I was extremely careful most of the time outside of the factory, but I became a little lax while within the confines of the factory walls. We had a very classy shipping clerk that I became good friends with. She was probably in her 50s and I reminded her of her own son…until that time when I was relaying to her a problem with a shipment and I said "I don't know where that f*#@ing thing went!" I think that got me off of her inheritance list.

Author

MESSAGE FROM BEYOND

"Life Membership expires in less than a week."

I received the above announcement from Trout Unlimited the other day…do they know something I don't?

Author

If you are ever foreign tourist needing to know where to go in Salzburg, just follow the sign!

Author

PEONIES

Speaking of problems with the English language...I had a neighbor once in this category. He told me once as I was admiring his flowers, "Them peonies (pronounced pee-ō-nees) sure is pretty, ain't they?"

Author

I'M GOING...NOW

Before we begin there is one thing that needs to be mentioned, I was 15 years old and had just recently started visits from my monthly friend. I was still new to the warning signs my body was giving me during that time of the month.

This story begins one spring evening at Kmart while shopping with my mom, dad, sister Rachel and best friend Blair. While walking down the isles, looking at flip-flops, I experienced a sudden wave of pain in my stomach. It quickly ceased, and without thinking anything of it, we proceeded to checkout and headed out of the store. As we made our way down the long isle of cars, the sudden pain came over me again. I assumed this feeling was the same feeling I had last month when I was having menstrual cramps.

Once we reached the car I started getting warm, sweaty and felt a rumble in my stomach. At that moment I knew that these were not what I had felt last month. I looked at my parents with big eyes and matter-of-factly stated "I'm going...now." They both looked at me confused, and asked "Honey, where are you going?" Knowing that we only had moments to act, I blurted out "I need to go to the bathroom now!". My parents, now both annoyed, asked why I didn't go while I was in the store and told me I needed to go back in. In a fit of rage, and running out of time, I told them I wasn't going to make it that far. They gave me another option of going to a closer store and using the bathroom. I sharply stated "NO. I'm going now". Finally understanding the severity of the situation, my dad, in all his wisdom, told me to "push up against the car". What he meant was press my rear-end against the side of the car preventing the inevitable. What I did, was maneuver around to the front of the car (you know, in that little space between your bumper and the bumper of the car in front of you) and proceeded to squat down and open the floodgates.

Feeling a little more relieved, but extremely embarrassed, I sat there for a minute allowing my stomach to empty. As if things couldn't get much worse, a bright light suddenly lit up the scene. There I was, face to face with the headlights of the car parked in front of ours. Slowly, they began to back up and pull away. Shocked, and even more embarrassed, I slowly began to stand and pull up my pants just in time to realize some of the boys from my class were walking past the now open parking spot. I couldn't be more humiliated.

Did I mention there was no TP available in the parking lot? I'm not sure what my best friend, my sister Rachel, and my dad were doing while this was happening, but when I got in the car, they were all smiles. My mom, however, insisted that I sit on my hip so I wouldn't press anything into her car seat.

With the windows down, and hands over their noses, we exited the parking lot in silence and made our way home.

We didn't make it more than a mile down the road before my sister, a frequent "chunk-blower", began to vomit out the window from the smell. She was seated in the middle of me and Blair, which meant that she had to lean over Blair to get the window. She certainly wasn't going to lean my direction. My mom pretty quickly realized the situation was going from bad to worse and emptied a shopping bag for Rachel to use. Little did Rachel and my mom know, the shopping bag had a few small holes in the bottom, and began to leak.

Panicking as the smells began to mix and realizing her bag was dripping, Rachel was looking for the quickest way to get the bag out of the car - the window. As we all know, it isn't easy tossing something from a moving vehicle, let alone a flimsy plastic bag full of puke. The bag flew back in the car, just as quickly as it went out, leaving some of us streaked in Rachel's dinner.

We eventually made it home and Rachel and I went straight into the shower, not bothering to remove our clothes. Blair proceeded to help my parents clean out the car without a word. Best friends like these are hard to come by. To this day, I can't walk into a Kmart without reliving these moments.

Mallory O., Culver City, CA

HOLLIS AND CASSANDRA

In the early 1970s, my wife and I moved to Connecticut for my first job and for my wife to attend college. We ended-up in central Connecticut, very near a prestigious private university. Because we were dirt poor, we used the university as our main source of entertainment. It was very obvious to many of the students that we just did not belong, and sometimes they let us know that. The university had some very wealthy, quite snobby students. Coming from the Midwest, our impression was of very wealthy students, all recently graduated from east coast boarding schools. The term "WASP" was probably coined after someone visited this campus in the 70s.

That first year we were excited to be able to attend the pre-graduation ceremony concert, outside in a beautiful part of the campus on a beautiful spring day. We sat on an amphitheater-style hillside overlooking the concert and enjoyed the beginning of the concert. Within a few minutes, a WASP-ish couple, let's call them Hollis and Cassandra, arrived to much fanfare (at least in their minds) and parked themselves right in front of us. They had checked us out and knew we shouldn't be there, but felt satisfied with a non-verbal disapproval and proceeded to set themselves on their Burberry blanket.

Cassandra sat down in her very lady-like manner while Hollis stood, better able to block us from viewing what we were not entitled to see. Cassandra had on an appropriate summer dress, properly tucked under her legs such that no improper view was granted to those below her on the hillside. Hollis had on the uniform of the day, which was a Brooks Brothers matched WASP outfit that included linen pants, a pink oxford shirt, an ascot (yes, an actual ascot), a dark blue blazer and, of course, his penny-loafers since this was a casual affair.

Cassandra sat and sipped ice tea taken from a perfect wicker basket, while Hollis stood perfectly erect, hand on hip, pinky finger out, sipping the Heineken poured perfectly into a chilled glass. My wife and I had several good chuckles at their expense, then settled in to watching the concert. After a short while, my eye was attracted to the right. A mongrel dog was working its way along the hillside through the crowd trying to snatch food from people as they watched the concert. Nearly everyone caught him in the act or saw him coming soon enough to shoo him away. Everyone, that is, except Hollis and Cassandra.

The dog came up on them from behind. By this time I had alerted my wife that something big was about to happen if this dog attempted to steal something from the basket. The dog, however, had a different idea. He sniffed Cassandra for a few seconds, unbeknownst to her, then lifted his leg and let fly with a ten second burst while she kept sipping her ice tea. The dog then moved over to Hollis, sniffed again, and let go another burst on his beautiful slacks. By this time Cassandra had caught a glimpse of the dog and alerted Hollis that it was present. About then, she felt the wetness on her back and screamed. She then pointed out to Hollis that he had also been a victim. Needless to say, my wife and I were almost rolling down the hill in laughter as they looked at each other in mutual disgust, repacked their perfect basket and left, undoubtedly to go to the local Hilton to change.

The last we saw of the dog, it was running off to the left with a chicken leg in its mouth and another person in hot pursuit yelling at it.

Author

MY SLUTTY CAT

We have a cat that needs constant attention during its waking hours - all five hours per day. It is so social, so needy, that we refer to him as "the slut." On his first visit to a new but experienced veterinarian he was the model cat. The vet was amazed that a fully equipped cat with fangs and four-wheel drive claws posed such little risk throughout the first part of the exam. A constant purring and head butting greeted each element of the exam.

"Well I doubt he'll like this very much," said the vet as he prepared to deploy his rectal thermometer. The astonished cat received the instrument, looked up at him, and promptly resumed purring. With great conviction, the stunned and incredulous veterinarian managed to say, " I ...have...never...seen...that...before."

Steve W., St. Paul, MN

MONSIGNOR GAS

As a grade-schooler, I attended a Catholic school. As was unofficially required, I was an altar boy. One of the best gigs for an eighth-grade altar boy was a funeral during the school week. This meant not only getting out of school for an hour or two, but a usual $5 pay-off for serving at the funeral – a double benefit.

One morning we got the call for a couple of boys and it was my turn in the rotation. My partner, let's call him Tom because it was so long ago that I have long since forgotten which of the many other altar boys it was, and I celebrated this timely death and jubilantly marched over to the adjacent church and got on our robes, hoping that the funeral celebrant (always a strange term to use for this function) was not our grumpy old German monsignor. We proceeded with the pre-mass arrangements of lighting candles, putting out the various items needed for the ceremony, like the water, wine and incense, while waiting for the priest to arrive.

Very shortly before the funeral was to begin, in walked the Monsignor, much to our chagrin. It seemed very out of character for this stringent, timely German-bred man to be almost late, but we hurried and got into our line and went into the altar area to begin.

We began with the traditional solemnity required for such a sad time, and repeated our Latin responses to all of the Monsignor's intros. About 15 minutes into the mass, the Monsignor let fly with a double-whammy fart that caused both Tom and I to break out in an instantaneous and audible chuckle. Unfortunately, the chuckle was a little louder than the fart, which only Tom and I could hear. No sooner had we settled down a bit, then another string let fly. Imagine the setting and the absolute requirement to stifle a laugh, then experiencing another round after gaining a modicum of control. Again we had trouble hiding the giggles. This time the

Monsignor slightly turned his head and said "Quiet!" I don't know about Tom, but I felt like saying "You too!" – of course that would have meant that me and my entire family would have been excommunicated and probably sent to Purgatory or Limbo or some such Catholic fate immediately.

Things went from bad to worse very quickly. Part of the Catholic funeral service was to go down and bless the casket with holy water and incense. I was the incense boy and Tom had the holy water. Tom went first as I watched in horror as he fought his giggles all the way around the casket in full view of the grieving family. I was a few feet in the background fighting the laughter with all of the resolve I had available, which turned out not to be enough. My turn came and I broke out in an audible chuckle a couple of times and converted it immediately, at least I thought it was that fast, into a cough. I don't think anybody bought that. I could not make eye contact with any of the funeral attendees for fear that I would break out into the full belly-shaking uproarious laughter that was hiding ever so close to escape.

After an eternity, longer for us it seemed than that about to be experienced by the deceased, the funeral ended and the face-to-face with Monsignor had arrived. We walked into the vestibule and noticed that the Monsignor took his robes off especially fast and was heading for the door quickly. As he passed us and we got ready, all he said was "Disgusting boys. Disgusting!" and he left. Tom and I both said "We're sorry Monsignor", but he was long gone. By this time we were all laughed out and couldn't muster that laugh we knew would bring us down as good Catholic boys doing our duties. I'm not sure if it was the Monsignor or the offended family, but we never received our $5 for this funeral. It was worth it, though, because I have a memory that brings me to laughter still, almost 50 years after it happened.

Author

The ultimate in "green" cemeteries—no resource wasted.

Author

JIM'S LEECHES

Ribbon leeches (not "bloodsuckers") are used for walleye fishing. My brother Jim's friend, Gary (no, not that one), hated leeches. He'd open the chip dip style container and set it on the boat seat in front of him. He'd then hold the fishing line about four inches above the hook, and try to get a leech out of the container by getting one "draped" over the hook. This usually took approximately five full minutes. Those five minutes provided the other leeches with an opportunity to make a break for it. Gary would then decide to simply use one of the escapees as his bait. Once the container was covered, Gary would proceed to chase the leech around the boat seat and try and poke the hook through the slippery, wiggling escapee without actually touching it with his fingers. Of course, every time the leech felt the hook, it would recoil away. After about ten more minutes of "pin the hook on the leech", Gary was usually fishing.

The second or third year Gary was with us for our traditional opening weekend fish-a-thon, Jim bought a dozen leeches, and a dozen hooks with short lengths of line already tied to the hooks. He then sat in the parking lot of the bait shop and hooked each leech onto each hook, and put the cover back on. Out in the boat, Jim watched Gary's arduous ritual of pin the hook on the leech. After Gary finally succeeded, Jim casually reached back for his special container of bait – a dozen neatly arranged lines sticking out from beneath the cover. He popped the lid off, and nonchalantly removed one line with hook and leech all ready to go. When Gary asked what he had, Jim told him he decided to splurge and buy his leeches "pre-hooked" which saved both time and effort. Gary not only believed him, but when he got to shore, he insisted on driving back to the bait store so HE could buy some pre-hooked leeches too!

We never did hear how his argument went as he insisted that the bait shop owner sold pre-hooked leeches, but both of us would have loved to hear him make his case.

TC, St. Paul, MN

HUGE BLOOD SUCKER

While heading out fishing, my brother and I saw an enormous blood sucker (not ribbon leech) swimming along. This was a one-of-a-kind specimen about a foot long when swimming. These, for the uninitiated, are the mushy, soft, slimy predators that cling to any living thing. They gnaw an opening in the skin (their mouths craftily containing an anesthetic so you don't notice them), and gorge themselves on the host's blood.

My 15 year old nephew (Phil) was deathly afraid of them. In the interest of science and surprise, I scooped it out of the water and put it in our leech container for Phil to find later.

After we returned from fishing, as usual, I put the leech container back in the fridge. The cold keeps them fresh and lively by reducing oxygen consumption. This one became so lively it was able to push the lid of the container enough to escape. It fell through the refrigerator shelf and landed directly into the Waldorf salad my sister-in-law made to have with dinner. Looking for a way out, it proceeded to make several laps in the bowl. These laps were evidenced by the inch-wide grey ring of slime in the salad.

Fortunately, most of us were outdoors when my sister-in-law discovered the blood sucker doing laps in her salad. Hearing loss from the scream was limited to my wife, and a couple stray dogs in the area.

TC, St. Paul, MN

Y2K

Just before the big Y2K scare, I worked for a public planning agency. We all received a memo from on-high a few weeks before January 1, 2000 pertaining to the possibilities of disaster when that fateful day occurred. From December 20th through January 6th all leaves and vacations were cancelled, and no one could be out sick without a doctor's permission slip.

When the first day of mandatory attendance arrived, we were all in our places, in compliance with the directive from above – with two exceptions: my boss and his boss (the originator of the memo). They took the day off.

Author

SOME ASSEMBLY REQUIRED

Wife #1 was a girl from a small college town. Her dad was a mechanic, and like a lot of the locals, always leery of "those college people" – professors in particular.

One day I saw a professor from the U walking down the sidewalk with a terrible limp, and his hand bandaged up. I asked my father-in-law what happened to the professor. "His new lawn mower got him", he said. The word was the guy bought the lowest priced mower he could find, and was so cheap he wouldn't pay to have it assembled. This was the most basic of mowers. No automatic rewind; no throttle; and no on/off switch. To turn it off, one had to reach down and push a metal reed-shaped tab against the spark-plug to short out the ignition system.

The professor got the thing home, and began his assembly project. Apparently, he thought he didn't have time for or need the instructions. After bolting the wheels on; latching the handle on; he filled the gas tank and was ready to go. Problems began with the starter rope. It threads through a handle-sized block of wood and is supposed to have a knot on each end. The flywheel of the mower has a slot designed to accept the knotted end of the rope. As you pull the rope, it automatically disengages from the flywheel. Having ignored the instructions, the professor tied the rope to the flywheel.

His foot firmly planted on the mower deck; wooden handle solidly in hand; our hapless professor gave a mighty pull. As luck would have it, the mower started on the first pull. Remember it has no throttle? It just runs full speed, or not at all. Full speed means about 3,500 rpms. Remember the rope tied to the flywheel? It too goes 3,500 rpms. Remember the wooden handle on the end of the rope? Speed? 3,500 rpms. That's how many times per minute it could whack someone in the shin. For those interested, 3,500 rpms is nearly SIXTY whacks per second!

Having been whacked in the shin sixty or more times, the professor reached down to shut off the mower. Remember the metal reed-shaped tab that shorts out the spark plug? Yup, our professor reached down with his bare hand to press it against the spark plug. Normally this is a safe enough thing to do, but this was anything but normal. He had a wooden handle flying around, right above the spark plug, at sixty whacks per second.

As my highly experienced mechanic father-in-law watched the professor hobble down the street, clutching his broken hand, he said, "you know, I think some people are just too over-educated for their intelligence".

TC, St. Paul, MN

GRANDMA AND THE METRIC SYSTEM

My grandparents immigrated from Germany shortly after World War I. They worked hard to learn to read and write English. It didn't occur to me that they had to learn the English system of measurements, as well.

In the early 1980s, the U.S. was considering switching over to the metric system. By that time, my Grandpa was gone and my Grandma was living alone in a small cabin on a lake in northern Minnesota. The only year-round neighbors she had were half a mile away. The others were only around on the weekends.

Outside one day, she and I got talking about the proposed change to the metric system. I had no idea it would upset her. She immediately pulled her 80-year-old self up to her full 4 feet, 10 inches, and told me exactly what she thought. She said, "Ven ve come here, ve learn da English writing. Ve learn da English speaking. I haf to change all da dress patterns and such from da Metric to da English. Now day vant me to change it back!"

Despite being in the middle of nowhere, she carefully looked over her shoulders to make sure there wasn't anyone around and said, "Vell, I'm not doin' it!!" I think that was the first time I ever heard or saw her stand up to the government. Given where she came from, I'm guessing it took more courage than I gave her credit for.

TC, St. Paul, MN

TRY THAT AGAIN

While answering my wife's inquiry about how much our car weighed, I indicated it was about a ton and a half. She was amazed that it was close to 8,000 pounds – she was convinced a ton was 5,280 pounds.

Author

Horses do the darnedest things…my son on a rental steed.

Author

THE PUNKIN COLLECTION

Our friend Mary C. of Lakeville, MN has been called Punkin since childhood. I'm not sure whether it started as a nickname of fondness from her parents or because of her wonderfully red hair. The following three stories come from her.

Orange Hair

Okay, so I'm getting older day by day. I admit it – I color my hair. I used to have my husband do this for me with the hair color I purchased from the drug store. Once, as Tom was in a bit of a hurry, I rushed to the bathroom to prepare the dying kit. I snipped the tip off the bottle top of the dye and poured it into the other solution bottle. Tom was right behind me, so he proceeded to patiently put the dye in my hair, starting on the top where the gray is the most prevalent.

As I'm a redhead, the color always comes out a little "off", but it usually gets better after the first washing, so I thought nothing of it when the color was a bit more orange than usual. The next day, I was scheduled to work ticket-sales at my daughter's lacrosse game. I sat out in the sun collecting money for over an hour. After that, I sat for a couple hours in the bleachers watching the game. By the time the game was over, Tom commented that my hair seemed kind of streaked. I blew off the comment – what does he know???

When I got home, I was shocked! My hair was not only striped - it was a completely different color on top than anywhere else, and that color was a monkey-butt orange – not a pretty sight! Washing only accentuated the orange on the top. When I thought back on what could have gone wrong, I couldn't quite remember if I had actually mixed the dye and second solution – which means all the concentrated dye went right on top of my head. The sun did its job and showed the world how I had messed up. Needless to say, I now get my hair colored professionally.

Dorm Pranks
1969: While in college, during finals, you just plain need a "release" from all the pressure of studying. Sophomore year, my roommate Cathy and I thought we'd have some fun with our best friends next door in the dorm, Kris and Sandy. One day while they were out of their room, I went in and hid a spool of thread in a bin on the floor of Kris' closet. As the closet was right next to the door, it was easy to then pull the end of the thread out the doorway and into our room. When Cathy and I would need a break at night, we'd pull on the thread. This would apparently make all sorts of funny sounds come from Kris' closet because they would then come charging into our room screaming about the noises they were hearing. Cathy and I would be very supportive while they were in our room. The minute they left, however, we would explode with laughter. This went on for about a week before a really angry Kris showed up holding the spool of thread. We still thought it was absolutely hilarious, but we felt bad (sort of), and had to make amends to Kris for what seemed like a really long time.

To be fair, part of her anger stemmed from the week before the thread incident. Cathy and I had stacked pop cans outside Kris and Sandy's door. When I say "stacked", I mean we built a tower, and the whole door was completely covered. The idea was that, when they opened the door, the pop can wall would tumble in on them – funny, right? Well, just our luck – they opened the door, and the wall just stood there. Again, Cathy and I saw the humor. Kris and Sandy....not so much.

Friends

My friend Laurie and I try to get together for an hour every other week. We usually meet at Applebee's – it's close and convenient for us both. This is right after work (4:00), so we usually share an appetizer and a drink – yes, we share a drink. They're big! Sharing gets us both a good-sized glass, which is plenty!

One week, Laurie suggested we try Buffalo Wild Wings for a change. We met there and chatted for awhile before ordering. Laurie was telling me about how her hair no longer had any body. She didn't know if it was the cut or if her hair was changing. I sort of pulled up a piece of her hair to see how it was layered. When it came time to order, Laurie ordered one drink, told the waitress that we weren't very big drinkers, and said we would like to share a drink. Our appetizer came. Then, our drink arrived – ONE drink with TWO straws!!!! The waitress set it down and walked away. Laurie and I looked at each other and burst out laughing. We really like each other, but not that much! All we could figure out was that the waitress, seeing me touching Laurie's hair, assumed we were a couple. We politely asked for a second glass when the waitress returned. Just for good measure, though, before we left the restaurant, we hugged.

Mary C., Lakeville, MN

MUMMER'S SINGING

My mother (fondly called "mummer" by my father) suffers from the rages of dementia, which is a terrible affliction. However, there are times when she comes out with some pretty funny stuff. Once when I was visiting her, she fell asleep in her chair. Falling asleep is a great relief for my father because it is one of the few times he gets any peace and quiet because her dementia causes her to incessantly talk. She was out quite deeply when the Cubs baseball game came on. After the pre-game discussion, the National Anthem began. My mother, while still fully asleep, sang along with the Anthem in full voice, which is not a pretty thing. This is especially funny since she wouldn't have any idea what the words are or even what the song is if we would ask her. The next day we were sitting with my sister and her husband and I was relaying the story of the National Anthem while we watched a bit of that day's Cubs game. I'm not sure they appreciated the humor of it until the 7th inning stretch arrived and my mother, while sound asleep again, sang along to "Take Me Out to the Ballgame" while never leaving the depths of sleep.

Author

THE GOLF DAYS

I used to spend every Sunday morning during golf season out on the course with some good buddies. I was always the worst player of the group, but I generally had a good time anyway and enjoyed the camaraderie. I always felt like I was part of the foursome for comic relief. One of the Toms (there were two…both Tom C.) somehow acquired a pink putter that became the annual award for the funniest story of the year. I have long since stopped playing golf for the safety of all who might ever be on the same course, but I can remember a few of the annual winners.

Fore!

Perhaps the longest driver and hardest hitter of our group was an occasional guest named (yes) Jack Frost. Jack hit the ball long and well…most times. On one occasion, however, he somehow got behind the group, which was unusual because he was usually waiting for us to get up to where his ball was. The rest of us lost track of where he was because we simply weren't used to keeping track of him, as opposed to me who was forced to wear a cowbell. All of a sudden we heard a crack and a yell of "FORE!" Tom C. #1 was in the middle of the fairway about 50 yards down the fairway from Jack. Tom turned around to see where the ball was at the exact time the ball reached his forehead. His feet flew up in the air as his head flew downward and hit the ground…no additional movement. We all rushed over to see if we would need to move him to the side so we could finish our round and come back for him later, when he sat up with a huge two-inch "pimple" right between his eyes. What could have been a terrible disaster (not being able to finish our game) turned out OK, but remember when you hear FORE, do not turn to see why someone called it out. Jack won the putter that year.

The Dead Goose

The course we usually played had a ton of geese always around. One day a long string of them was walking across the fairway about 100 yards out of the tee box. This was a suitable distance since most of us could hit the ball over 100 yards even on a bad day. However…that same Tom C. #1 as above just happened to hit a low screamer about two feet off of the ground for about 101 yards right into the neck of one of those geese. The goose was not happy. Its neck hung at about a 45 degree angle as it went around in circles looking for whoever did this to him – he was genuinely pissed. Tom C. walked up, took a look and said "Ick", then walked away. I queried about his interest in putting this creature out of its misery, but he wasn't at all interested. As an act of mercy (which I hated by the way) I dispatched him with my putter – turns out geese have very strong necks and heads and this was much more difficult than I planned. I finally put it out of its misery and threw it in the rough. The next week we checked where I had thrown it and found only a beak and one of its feet. Tom C. #1 got the pink putter that year.

A Diverted Path
Although I'm sure I got the pink putter many times, the only time I can remember getting it was for my prowess with the driver. I drove off on a 300+ yard hole and put my ball on the green. Unfortunately, it was a green for another hole. I carefully removed my ball from the green and hit it again…landing on another green… again on the wrong hole. On my third try I hit the right green, and walked away with that year's honors…three tries to get on the right green

180°
I can't short-change Tom C. #2, who actually initiated the pink putter tradition - I think to humiliate others because he was usu-

ally a good player. On a short over-the-water par three, he actually hit such a slice that it went into the air, curved back so far to the right that it landed in the pond right next to us – a perfect 180° arc from the tee box. Bingo – pink putter for you!

Author

Go out and play kids...don't worry about those wires (note the "playground" on the tower pad).

Author

THE VACUUM CLEANER

When our old vacuum cleaner was wearing out, wife #2 asked if I'd be willing to research and buy a new one. After shopping around for styles and prices, I ended up buying an upright instead of a canister-type like we had.

Upon bringing it home, my wife wanted a quick lesson on how to change settings, change the bag, etc. After filling her in on all of the features, I added that the salesperson was very insistent about using the vacuum correctly during the break-in period. I told her that because the bristles on the brush underneath the machine needed to take the correct "set", it was important to only move forward with the vacuum until the ten hour break-in period was over. No pulling the machine backward, only forward.

As she stood in the living room looking at the hallway and other rooms full of furniture, it was easy to see the wheels turning in her head as she plotted an imaginary course through the house pushing the vacuum, and never pulling it backward. Finally, she spoke up and said, "man, ten hours is a long time!" Even though I confessed before she got too far in trying it out, I barely avoided sleeping in the garage…I should have emphasized, this was ex-wife #2.

TC, St. Paul, MN

THE OLIVE

When I was in high school, a friend of mine thought of himself as quite the ladies man. Somewhere, he saw a foreign film that included two lovers passing a strawberry to each other as they kissed. He thought it was the coolest thing he'd ever seen.

At a party in someone's basement, he decided he'd try the sexy maneuver himself. When he kissed his girlfriend, he passed her a green olive. Unfortunately, he hadn't told her in advance. Apparently, she thought the tip of his tongue fell off. There was instantaneous projectile vomiting, closely followed by projectile questions.

TC, St. Paul, MN

ZIGGY

I grew up in Illinois, but my parents were both from Wisconsin. The practical result of this for a teenage boy was that I had a lot of cousins about my age located in a state where beer drinking was legal at age 18. While I was only 17 and out of state, I found that where there's a will, there's a way.

My cousin Bill (age 18) put together a scheme wherein I would use one of his buddy's driver's license one Saturday night. He would find a friend that looked vaguely like me and I would simply memorize all of the pertinent details on the driver's license and enjoy the rest of the night. Wisconsin being quite a melting pot of nationalities turned into a major obstacle to our plan. The buddy he tapped was named Zbigniew Drabowiecz. Try pronouncing, or worse yet, spelling that after a couple of beers!

Author

HAMBURGER

A friend of mine took her college-student daughter out for lunch. They decided to share the hamburger, fries, and dessert special. After explaining the plan to split the burger to the server, she asked the daughter "how would you like that done?" The daughter couldn't believe it, and answered "uh…, cut in half?"

TC, St. Paul, MN

ROD HOLDERS

I love fishing for muskies. They're big, the lures are cool, and casting to great-looking spots is fun. One year I decided to add rod holders to my boat in case I wanted to take a break from casting heavy lures, and just troll around the lake for a while. Besides, it was a good way to spend some garage time until fishing season started.

Positioning the rod holder was a little trickier than I anticipated. I wanted it close enough to reach easily from my seat, but not in the way of the boat's controls or steering wheel. The additional challenge was that the handles on heavy rods like I use are very long and could easily get in the way of the various controls.

After carefully measuring several times, I drilled the necessary hole and mounted the holder. To ensure that it wouldn't interfere with steering, or shifting gears, I gabbed one of the rods and placed it in its holder. I sat in the boat in the garage testing my handiwork – turning the steering wheel, shifting gears, running the throttle, grabbing for the rod like I would if I had a bite, etc. Suddenly, I had this uneasy feeling...there at the bottom of my driveway sat the mailman in his truck watching me "fish" in my garage. Although he politely waved, I saw him burst into laughter as he drove away.

TC, St. Paul, MN

AN ENGINEER'S TALE

[Author's note – This story is included not for its humor, which to me is evident, but for its "engineering style". Jack is an old friend – an engineer – who never was too concerned about spelling and grammar. "Who cares" is his attitude. I include this as I received it because it is a great example of why engineering schools should start all incoming freshman with a good English course. Have some fun and see how many of the spelling and grammatical errors you can spot or missing commas you would place!]

One spring when we were on our Robert trent Jones golf tour in Alabama we came upin a water hole. Being the spring time of the year geese were sitting on there nest. It was not a good day for me. I had about a 100 yard shot over the water. But low and behold I hit a worm burner right in the water pretty close to a mommy goose. I thought bnothing of it consideriing it was a fluck so I dropped anojther ball and preceeded to hit another ball into the water almost in exactly the same place. Well the Mommy goose was now getting pretty pissed and so was I. Dropping a third ball I agian hit it in the water and almost hit the goose. That was enough for me so I proceeded to the green in my cart but the path around the water pinched down and the goose came charging out at the cart. Luckily I was driving and my partner was on the wrong side with the goose as it almost took his leg off.

Another time also in Alabama Tom #2 was trying to get over the water and like in Tin Cup he kept hitting it in the watre. He kept sayibng I know I can clear the water and most have tried a half dozen times. Finally he realized in lieu of hitting a 6 iron he was hitting a 9 iron.

Jack F., Maplewood, MN

YEA OL' TIME FAMILY DRUG STORE

My father and I ran a neighborhood drug store in Pittsburgh. We were one of five drug stores within a two mile radius. The former owner was an old rum-runner, transporting booze in tires during Prohibition. He had several very colorful customers who continued to frequent our pharmacy, including a member of Al Capone's gang (Joe Staudi), who would raise his shirt, if asked, to proudly reveal a line of three small scars from a machine gun shooting. He was one of several narcotic addicts who would bring in legal prescriptions for a week's supply of morphine. Another such customer, a professional shoplifter, had outfitted his over-coat or rain-coat (depending on the season) on the inside with an assortment of hooks and various sized pockets. We even had a mammoth cop, who, in the winter, found shelter in our store. He hated the cold and became just one of the fixtures, spending hours daily out of the cold and snow.

Our most picturesque employee was Mickey, a slightly alcoholic, wounded, WW II disabled veteran. He was our merchandise stocker, delivery man, floor mopper, general repairman and comic relief. Mickey felt that if you drank enough beer, you would never contract cancer. This belief, however, did not save him from a premature death from cancer.

One very hot summer day, when the shelves were dusted and the deliveries made, Dad, unable to put up with Mickey doing nothing, sent him down through a trap door in the back to straighten up the stock cellar. It was at least 105 degrees down that hole that day. After an hour or two, Dad looked down the stairs to call Mickey up to take out a delivery. Suddenly I hear Dad scream "MICKEY, WHAT THE HELL ARE YOU DOING!!!" I came charging over, peered down, and there was Mickey, pouring sweat, with his fly open and his ample manship hanging out. Mickey looked back up with a large grin, and said "Well, you make me work like a horse, I may as well look like one!"

Dad, ever serious, would never crack a smile, let alone laugh at one of Mickey's antics, just threw him a long suffering, wry, head-shaking look. Mickey and I burst out laughing, and did so all day whenever we looked at each other.

Jerry F., Tustin, CA

While traveling in Europe a few years ago, I got off a tour bus and was a slight bit confused which one it was upon my return. After looking at the back of this bus, I knew it was the one. I had to translate from Danish, which I can't speak, but after some thought I realized that this bus was oversized (www must be the European equivalent of EEE) and was "Here, for the large tourist fart (assumedly the Americans on it)." As for the .dk, I just don't know. But I knew I had found my place.

Author

When a sign says it all…

Author

BRITISH MUMS

Following are a few stories about British mums, a group that spans a broad range, and is always fun to talk about.

Me Scottish Mum
My Scottish mother was in line at a store behind a very prim and

proper, snobbish older woman. In Scotland, many of the small stores have various materials in storage behind the counter, so the older woman asked the person behind the counter for some toilet tissue. The sales person asked "Would you like that it in roles or in sheets?" The older woman then said "On the (w)hole, it doesn't make much difference, does it?" My mother slapped the old bag on the back and said "Good one! It really doesn't matter to the ol' bum, does it?"

John T., Lake Forest, CA

My English Mother-In-Law

#1 — My mother-in-law is very British. Like the late Queen mum whom she adored, she finds "a wee bit of gin" to be a nice way to relax. One evening we were on our neighbor's patio enjoying a small bonfire and the gin and tonic mastery of Randy (the homeowner). Randy makes his G&Ts in plastic stadium cups that hold about 12 fluid ounces after accounting for ice. These are big drinks.

After two of these monsters everybody is in a pretty good mood, especially my 75-yr old mother-in-law. She shook her cup while peering in it--the international symbol for "refill please." Glances are exchanged all around and Randy dutifully headed inside to conjure up several more. My wife, now inside too, pleads with him to go easy on the gin this time. The master pauses, torn between continued excellence and public safety. He eventually agrees to weaken the drink.

Out on the deck our hero receives her drink, sips it, and immediately says, "Oh Rahhnndee,"- she says it like his name is the adjective--"not your best effort dear."

Steve W., St. Paul, MN

My English Mother-In-Law
#2 — My mother-in-law is oh so British and proper. And like most English mothers, she has a way of cutting her children down to size with a few well-chosen words. During a recent visit she was perched at the kitchen table, enjoying her morning tea while I did my best to recall the etiquette involved in consuming peanut butter toast while half asleep.

My wife is a business executive who dresses the part nicely, decided to join us. She walked in wearing a sharp Jones of New York business suit obviously cognizant of the fact that her mother would likely approve. Instead, all she heard was, "Oh Susan, you have so many nice things you could have worn."

Steve W., St. Paul, MN

GITTYUP

After our mixed doubles bowling, our partners Charlie and Kathy came over for drinks. They were in their mid to late 30's at the time, and had been married for years. Although only a year apart in age, Charlie was a big guy; bald; a little heavy; and frankly looked older than he was. Kathy on the other hand was a petite;

cute blond; who looked younger than her 35 years.

Charlie also like to dress in western style shirts; big belt buckle; and cowboy boots and hat.

As we talked and laughed, we finally noticed my 4-year-old son would look Charlie up and down; go look out the window; then back to Charlie; then back to the window. Finally he stopped in front of Kathy. His eyes wide with anticipation, he asked, "Did your dad ride his horse?!"

Charlie never lived it down.

TC, St. Paul, MN

A.J. AT THE WHEEL

I don't know why, but funny stories always seem to come in threes as I recall them. My father, A.J., not to be confused with the great racecar driver A.J. Foyt, as you will discover, wasn't a bad driver – he was just a bit distracted.

His first misfortune was caused by me at a pretty young age. I had just learned a cute new word for the police that I was itching to use. As we drove along in Wisconsin on our way to a vacation, I spotted a police car on station and hidden slightly behind some trees. I yelled out "Look at the fuzz!" My father, of course, turned to look and proceeded to run right through a stop sign. The flashing red lights came on and A.J. received a memento of that trip.

Many years later, my father was upset with all of the speeders on our street and called the local sheriff requesting that something be done about it. Shortly thereafter, a 30 mph speed limit sign appeared on our street. However, the speeding continued, so my father called and again demanded that something be done. The next afternoon while he was at work, a squad car showed up with a radar gun. You probably guessed it, but the first person they apprehended that day was A.J. as he drove up the hill after work.

My father, as I previously mentioned, was easily distracted when he drove. His bobble-head seemed as though it was everywhere but straight ahead on the road. One day he ran over to the local carry-out chicken restaurant during the Christmas season to get dinner for the family. He seemed as though he had been gone a long time, when the phone rang. My mother listened a while, then said "Oh, A.J." She sent my brother two streets over to retrieve the chicken for dinner while my father arranged for his car to be towed…he had been looking at Christmas decorations in the neighborhood on the way back from the restaurant and slammed into a car parked at a neighbor's house to attend a Christmas party. He apparently was trying to look at the party through their large front window as he drove, with a not unexpected result.

Author

AN ADVENTURE

Ah, to be young and carefree. It was October, 1971. We had been married since June and were living in Washington, D.C., where I was finishing up my two years of military duty after graduating from college.

My wife worked late on Fridays at her finance company job, so I typically picked her up when she got off at 8:00 and we'd splurge on a meal out. This Friday night, though, I had something different in mind. "How'd you like to go to Homecoming this weekend?" She thought that was a great idea, so we hurried home, packed a suitcase and started out an hour later on the over 800-mile drive to Carlinville, Illinois. Driving straight through the night, alternating shifts behind the wheel, we were about ten miles from the goal when we heard an ominous sound. It was the muffler dragging on the ground. We pulled over and with some help from a passing driver we were able to get the muffler disconnected. We rolled into town about 11:30 Saturday morning with a decision to make. Should we head right to campus or try to get the muffler fixed? We opted for the muffler but alas, no service station in our small college town stocked one. Oh, well, nice try.

We roared off to campus and found our best friends, visited for a bit and made arrangements to meet later that evening for drinks and dinner. Meanwhile, we'd grab a nap. Of course, deciding at the very last minute to make the trip meant we did not have reservations. And this being Homecoming weekend in a two-motel town, what were we thinking?

We cruised over to the first place and found that all the rooms were taken – no big surprise. Headed over to the second motel. Luck was with us; a construction worker had decided to go home for the weekend and his room was available. A motel bed never felt better. It was now about 2 in the afternoon. We figured we'd sleep till about 6:00 PM, get cleaned up and go meet our friends. A good plan, but we didn't wake up until 2:00 AM!!! We either did not set the alarm or slept through it. We missed the entire Homecoming event! We had driven for over thirteen hours for less than an hour of time with our friends. Crazy.

Now that we were awake, we pondered starting out for home or getting a few more hours sleep and heading out by 6 or 7 in the morning. We were starving but there was no place to get anything to eat in the middle of the night, so we chose the extra sleep. This time the alarm woke us, we grabbed a few donuts at the bakery in town and started our trip back to DC.

And without a muffler, it was a miserable trip. It was cold outside, and raining much of the way, but we felt we had to leave a window open to avoid the danger of exhaust fumes inside the car. The car sounded terrible so we slowed down through any towns or any time a police car got near us. Being pulled over for excessive noise was not how we wanted to cap off this adventure. We got back to DC late Sunday night and went to work on Monday morning with stories to tell.

Ah, to be young and carefree!

Tori and Cliff S., Tustin, CA

DOOR COUNTY FISHING

I never liked going out on the boat with my wife's Uncle Fran for those marathon fishing trips. Once you were out in the boat on Lake Michigan, he wouldn't go back to shore for anything less than death, and then he would want to throw out a few more casts. The first summer I spent up in Door County with my wife, her mom and dad, and Uncle Fran and Aunt Mae, is one I will always remember. Fran had a 40 foot fishing boat (more like a yacht to this city boy) and would arrange all day fishing trips out of Sturgeon Bay. I believe it was probably the second time out when I got real sick and (tried to) lay quietly inside the cabin. I couldn't tolerate Dramamine tablets to prevent seasickness because it was like a sleeping pill to me. So the crew (including my wife) was catching more fish than was possible while I tried everything to keep my nausea at a minimum. The SMELL!. They caught twenty-five fish that day. Of course, Fran invited every relative in town for a famous Door County fish boil that night. I learned how to skin fish that evening and I will never forget the SMELL. As the guests arrived and I met some of my wife's relatives for the first time, I waited for the opportunity to slip out of site and went down to a local restaurant for a cheeseburger. My biggest mistake was bringing it back to Uncle Fran's cabin where the act was not taken too fondly by the locals. Future summers in Door County were spent on the golf courses, thank you. People tell me that catching twenty-five fish on one trip is like hitting the lottery. I guess I have a different opinion on that thought!

Bill S., Rockford, IL

LOOK OUT BELOW

In 1946 Mom & Dad, shortly after they were married, ran a restaurant in Somonauk, Illinois, just outside Chicago on busy Highway 34. The restaurant was also a Greyhound bus stop and because of that, the restaurant was often slammed with whole busloads of hungry passengers. I was about six years old, my stepbrother Terry was five. We stayed behind the restaurant in a teeny trailer and when the restaurant wasn't busy, we helped out by getting French fries ready for the cooker. On the property were several peach trees and one day Terry ate a bunch of them. Unfortunately, the peaches were not quite ripe, so many trips to the bathroom ensued. The problem was that the only available bathroom was in a filling station adjacent to the restaurant, one also used by the bus stop patrons. We were told specifically not to use that facility while a bus was at the restaurant. But because of all the peaches he had eaten, Terry spent an abundance of time in the bathroom that day. After he had been gone for a while, I vividly remember seeing Terry streak across the back of the property, his romper suit in hand screaming and crying at the top of his voice! A rather large – OK very fat - woman had come into the bathroom, hadn't seen Terry because it was rather dark and proceeded to sit right down on the poor kid. To this day, Terry and peaches still don't mix!

Lori K., Trinidad, CO

JUMP...NOW!

In 1968 I taught school In Jackson, Wy. I skied often at Teton Village Ski area close to Jackson Hole. One morning I decided to take a quick run by myself, so I boarded the high speed lift ready for my run. On the way up the slope, I encountered someone in a chair coming down – not the usual route down the slope. I yelled over to the hapless woman "What happened?" She tearfully replied" I forgot to get off!" I hoped that the person at the top running the lift reminded the person at the loading ramp that there was someone coming down. I went on my run and later in the day, as I was eating lunch, I heard someone say that a woman came down a lift, and she, her skis and all, went around the bull wheel at the loading ramp (in a tiny little shed) at the bottom of the lift. There is NO spare room in there at all and how she managed to pull up her skis to get around the wheel, I can only speculate. I hear she wasn't hurt, but imagine the surprised lift operator when the chair came out of the lift house already loaded with a passenger, probably in the tucked position!

Lori K., Trinidad, CO

THE COUPON GUY

Charlotte meant well. She really did. After all, we've been friends since the 5th grade. So when she called to tell me her "find" for me, I took her at her word.

She was happily married with thoughts that I should have the same – a great guy, so I listened to her review. She and Bill had known Bob for a long time but sadly now he was a middle aged widower. His credentials were note worthy: about my age, well educated (engineering degree from Cal Tech), retired and more than well situated financially. Plus he lived within 10 miles of me. Could she give him my number?

Yes, of course! He called. We met at Mimi's for lunch. By agreement, Dutch treat, with no expectations of anything but a first meeting chat. Bob was tall, masculine with the lean look of a long time tennis player and liked to travel. What a nice guy she had pointed in my direction.

He called again to invite me to dinner. I accepted. We agreed on time, not place. He arrived with flowers picked from his garden. Very sweet, I thought. Since he'd not asked about my preference for food or a special restaurant, I assumed he had a surprise waiting.

He did. He drove to a Sizzler, fished out his "two for one coupon" telling me on the way in about what a great deal they offered on a steak and lobster combo. I don't eat lobster but rather than tell him that, I said I'd probably order a salad.

He stopped in his tracks, leaving me on the sidewalk, took an about face and ran back to the car for his discount coupon for salads.

Suddenly, the sparkle dimmed on the diamond.

Anne D., Irvine, CA

THE POPPING OF A BALLOON

One of the things I miss most about getting older is that I don't get those little looks anymore from pretty women as they pass. There are occasional glances by older ladies, but even those are few and far between. It is just one of life's little pleasures to exchange innocent glances and a little smile. It was with a little surprise, then, a few years ago when a beautiful young sales woman at a model home caught my eye because she kept staring at me. I was with my wife, but chose not to call it to her attention – rather I just sat back and enjoyed the attention and patted myself on the back thinking I still had IT. After a few minutes, she headed in my direction, keeping her eyes locked on me. I got a little nervous at this point wondering what she had in mind. As she approached close enough to reach out and touch my arm – and me almost hyperventilating – she said, "Excuse me for staring, sir, but you really remind me of my father." To make it even more humiliating, it turns out I knew her father. I was really disappointed to hear she thought I looked like him.

Author

STORIES FROM A FORMER TOUR CONDUCTOR

Jaclyn K. was in the tourist business for many years. She led tours all around the world and had many very interesting things happen to her, some of them funny. Here is a sample collection of her humorous encounters.

Missing in Translation

During the 1960s, I did a lot of traveling as a tour conductor. After nearly four years I decided to award myself the gift of a trip around the world the other way, going east, alone. On the first leg of my trip, I sat next to a friendly young man who had just finished his medical residency in a Boston. He was returning to his homeland, Panama, to set up his medical practice. After some conversation, he asked me what kind of work I did.

I replied, "I am a tour conductor."

He asked me if there was much demand for that in America. I responded that there was a lot of demand for it.

His reply: "In Panama, I don't know of a single turkey doctor."

Mooning, Lion Style

As a conductor taking groups of tourists – mostly seniors – to foreign countries, I saw a lot of humor.

On one African safari, we drove across the Serengeti plains in land rovers in search of lions. Suddenly, we heard "Look, Look! There's a lion." It was ahead of us across a dry clearing. The lion was walking nonchalantly right in front of us. The tourists got their cameras out and squeezed through the sun-roof opening on top of the rover, all focusing on the lion. The lion stopped, stooped down and proceeded to do a number two right in front of this admiring crowd! The group gasped, and tried to cover embarrassment. After a minute, we recovered and agreed that it was "mooning, lion style".

Unnamed #1

One day our tour took us on a bus ride in Japan to a large department store – an enormous room filled with hand-crafted goods from local artists. My group fanned out in all directions to shop. As was my usual procedure, a local representative escorted us and translated when necessary. This time it was difficult to locate all of the members of our group when it was time to get back on the bus to leave. Our local guide remarked to me as he was looking for our little old ladies with gray hair wearing blue print nylon dresses that "they all look the same to me."

Unnamed #2

In Suva Micronesia, I heard the most original pick-up line I ever ran into. It was following a dinner at the hotel. I walked across the pool area from the dining room to my room. I was followed by a short, robe-clad man wearing a turban. He said to me: "Are you fertile?" It seems his wife was only bearing him daughters. He would pay $30,000 for a woman to bear him a son. I declined…

Unnamed #3

In Cambodia in the 1960s, the members of my group heard guns so we were eager to leave the next morning. At the airport at Phnom Penh, we were herded to a small plane. As the leader, I was approached by a guard wearing dirty camouflage fatigues, heavy boots, and carrying a large rifle. He said, "You, follow me!" I followed him to the back of a rickety building, with wooden sides and chicken wire partitions to his "private office."

He sat down, leaned back in his wooden swivel desk chair, put his feet on the desk and handed me a book. It was a thick, dog-eared, soiled book with torn pages. He said, "Do you really live like this in Hollywood?" The book was Danielle Steele's "Secrets of Hollywood", a rather trashy novel about life in southern California. Suspecting his intentions, I ran out the door, across the tarmac and up the stairs into our plane. One of the tour members was standing in the door to keep it open for me. I sat down, relieved as we flew out.

Unnamed #4

One time my 13 year-old son visited me in Moorea Tahiti, where Muk, Jay and Kelley – Newport Beach expatriates – had just bought the Hotel Bali Hai. They were concerned because the entire dining room was in an uproar. The guests were all complaining. It seems the boys had to entice the villagers to work at their hotel, so they hired the local leader of the village ladies, who barely spoke English, in order to get waitresses.

Eavesdropping revealed the problem. The leader followed the other waitresses to the kitchen. When they placed their orders, she would simply say "ditto." Everybody was getting the food others had ordered. Dilemma! She didn't want to be humiliated by admitting she did not speak English. The solution – they put her in charge as a supervisor. The tried and true American solution!

Jaclyn K., Newport Beach, CA

SHRINKS VS. THE PARACHUTE

When we first moved to California from the East Coast, I was ready for some bizarre California experiences. In fact, I relished the prospects. For example, when my first work party at my boss' house turned out to be a Jacuzzi party - clothing optional - I took the plunge. Such a different way to meet and get to know other mental health professionals: Joe, the psychiatrist; Mickey, my boss and psychologist; Ralph, the social worker; and Gary, the mental health worker (now a DO/PhD). This group, who I all got to know so thoroughly and abruptly, was to become the core of a larger adventure in the next year.

Someone, not I, had the great idea to do an "adrenaline run" to help ease the stress of working with a disadvantaged, seriously mentally ill population. Hang-gliding was decided upon quickly and about 12 co-workers signed on and we began to check it out. However, scientists as we all supposedly were, and dedicated to research, we discovered that first time deaths in hang-gliding were not uncommon. That fact seemed to dampen a few spirits.

On to parachuting! Research here (second hand, no primary sources) showed no recorded deaths for first timers. We would in fact be attached by "static line" to the plane such that after "departing" the plane and a 50-foot fall, the parachute would open on its own. (That only rarely failed we later learned.) Now were really excited, and got down to the business of planning. We found a local jump school in Lake Elsinor (CA). We would have a day of training and then all together make our jump out of the door of a DC-3 from a half-mile up. A date was set.

My wife was not as thrilled as I at the prospects of my adventure. Married about 8 years, I had gained back my "baby fat" that I had largely lost during the time I met and courted my wife. I was not, and never had been, athletic. Besides, we now had three children. "What are you thinking?!" was one of the milder things she said. But I told her the statistics and told her all about our extensive one-day training and all of the safety equipment (including a two-way radio). She was certainly glad I would not be packing my own chute! I would myself later wonder several times who would be packing mine.

As the day approached, an interesting psychological phenomenon occurred at work: half of our ranks turned against us. Not only had they resigned from the big adventure, they also vehemently went on about how crazy we were to whomever would listen. It was quite interesting and strange.

The day came. I was the driver of the 15-seat maxi-van. We drove two hours to our destination, hiding our tension, talking about those who deserted us, but not knowing what was ahead.

The jump school put the six of us together in a classroom with about a dozen other novices. The next three hours was spent in educating us about technique, then after lunch we had two hours of practice jumping and rolling from a four-foot ladder. Then we loaded into a big, hollowed-out plane with the door removed. It had a clothesline down the center to which we attached our static lines. When our turn came, we were told to sit down in the doorway and jump out over the target area. We learned in class the importance of landing near the target zone. We could do so (theoretically) by pulling little handles up above us to "steer", but we had to learn this technique in class rather than trial and error during the jump. Hitting the target area was essential, we were told, because on one side of the "X" was a shallow lake. They said you wouldn't want to land there. You'd think a shallow lake is a good thing to land in, but not the case. It appears that the parachute could land on top of you and has enough weight to sink with you in the middle of it as it goes down. Even if you're a good swimmer (I'm fair) and aptly and quickly disengage from the chute (remember, I'm not athletic, nor am I particularly dexterous), three-feet of water is a problem if you're trapped.

On the other side of the target zone, our drill instructor-type teacher explained, there were a bunch of 40-foot tall high tension electrical lines. You don't even want to imagine what our instructor said would happen there. By the way, our instructor did not seem as amused as we were at this. All consummate professionals, we giggled nervously throughout the morning, bursting out whenever we would look at each other, cross-talking like no good student should. But how do you keep down a guffaw after the guy in front of you describes that after you voluntarily jump from the plane, you may, for example, look up and see a "May West." This is when one chute line has intersected the whole chute, making two halves instead of a complete circle – this is not good. Let me not detail for you the various maneuvers one must endeavor to complete when encountering a May West, or the myriad other techniques to deal with the primary or secondary chute malfunctioning. What had we gotten ourselves into?!

The jump time had come. We were exhausted from our ladder

practice in the 95-degree heat. Then we were told a thermal had developed – an "up-wind" during which you cannot jump. We would all have to come back the next morning. HA! All six of us did, but only two from the rest of our class joined us. Unfortunately, the DC-3 would not fly with only eight jumpers. We would go up instead in a bi-plane, get out of the fuselage onto the wing, hold on to the struts, wait for the sign to jump, and simply step away from the plane when told to do so. Only one of us froze.

It wasn't me; it was my boss, Mickey. What would you expect after being warned to keep your hand tightly over the ripcord, 'cause if you don't and the chute opens accidentally, it will not just pull you out of the plane. Oh no, it flies out the side door, catches the wind and flies behind the plane, incidentally ripping the tail section off – an unpleasant way to dump all us novice parachutists out.

But Mickey was the third jumper. Ralph was first, and he glibly stepped out by putting his foot under the door and finding the little step on the underbelly of the fuselage. From this he flung himself up onto the wing and inched out a few feet away from the body of the plane. As the plane repositioned itself over the target, he readied himself and the jumpmaster shouted "jump!"

He did, and a few seconds after, the chute opened and he floated down. He was correcting well over the target, positioned to make a perfect landing. And it appeared that he did, at first. But he didn't move from the site. He didn't roll, jump up and collect his chute. Instead, he just lay there. And a few guys ran over to help him, and he limped off with them.

Mickey saw that, and I guess it did something to her unconscious. She wanted to get into position with all her will—you could tell—but her body was frozen. The jumpmaster has apparently encountered this before, so he asked if she wanted his help. She resolutely nodded, and he reached over and grabbed her by the straps, putting her down in the doorway. She was able to do the rest all on her own.

The plane had pulled away to reposition. It was my turn.

I pulled myself through the cramped quarter, held onto the door-way as I groped for that little step. I then took the biggest leap of faith in my life. And I got onto that wing and held on for dear life. I couldn't believe how strong those winds were. I could hear nothing, not even the jumpmaster.

But somehow he got my attention, and when I saw him wildly gesticulating towards me, I guess I let go, because I was plung-ing. And not gracefully. I don't know whether I arched my back, counted to assure the chute opened or engage my back-up, or not. I blacked out briefly, but came-to to find myself swinging beneath the canopy. My chest strap was hitched up to my nose (I guess I hadn't cinched up enough), and I really couldn't see down.

But I got there in about two minutes, as predicted when your chute opens in time (as opposed to eleven seconds when not). I had rolled on landing, but I still felt like a sack of potatoes. I was able to get up on my own, with very wobbly knees. They walked me over to Ralph, who had a slight cut on his nose. We then watched together as Gary's chute opened above.

The ride back home was uneventful, except for the brief stop at the ER to check out one strained knee. We had done it. Six survived our first jump. How can one be exhilarated and so exhausted at the same time!

Stan S., Huntington Beach, CA

Kids' Art – Sometimes those pictures that come home from school are just too funny to toss. Do you ever wonder what the teachers think when they see these? Do they keep a collection?

Author

FOURTH OF JULY INCIDENT

On a 4th of July some 52 years ago, my husband, two daughters and I attended a fireworks program at a local park near where we lived in Santa Monica, California. It was a cool evening with a breeze, which necessitated my wearing the suede jacket I had brought along.

We had also brought a box of sparklers to enjoy. Of course, mommy wanted to participate in the fun and proceeded to strike a match to light a sparkler. The breeze foiled that plan (which I attempted several times).

With the usual resourcefulness I employed, I opened my jacket, lit my sparkler and drew it inside close to my left breast to shield the flame, whereupon my daughter screamed, "Mom!" alerting my husband to my idiotic solution to my intended pleasure of watching my sparkler in all its intended delight.

Needless to say, the moment was destroyed as I almost performed an instant and almost complete mastectomy on myself! After all these years, my family still hasn't lost the humor they felt at my foolishness.

Frances S., Irvine, CA

DISNEYLAND FRIGHT

This incident occurred some 53 years ago when I took my daughters, ages three and nine for a fun day at Disneyland. We were walking along Main Street when we decided to visit a "Babes in Toyland" exhibit that depicted various scenes from the movie. As we strolled along, we found ourselves in an extremely dark forest within a simulated forest scene.

Suddenly, my three-year old screamed with fright. I turned around to see an enormously tall tree hovering menacingly close to her.

In an instant, my motherly protectiveness, all 90 pounds of it, jumped into action and I accosted the tree (with the obvious human inside) and ranted and raved at it for having frightened my child.

There followed not one sound from the tree. I surely must have ruined the day for the employee inside who was, no doubt, hired to "delight" the kids by giving them a good scare. Do you think?

Frances S., Irvine, CA

HALLOWEEN SNOWSTORM

Anyone who lived in Minnesota that year will never forget the Great Halloween Snowstorm of 1991. Even after 50 winters in Minnesota, it's the one I recall most clearly – and there have been some real doozies. (There was another massive snowstorm on

Thanksgiving that year, but that's another story.) The Halloween Snowstorm is most memorable, I think, because it came out of nowhere, practically without warning, and left 30 – count 'em – 30 inches of snow in its wake when all was said and done.

The month had been fairly average, as I recall, with cool nights and warm, sunny days. No one was thinking much about winter the day before the snowstorm, and no one was ready for it. The leaves had only just begun falling from the trees, for example, and no one had made their cars ready for winter, and "remembered" from the previous winter how to drive in snow.

And then came the snow – truly a surprise, coming several weeks before a normal "early snow" might fall. And fall it did… and fall and fall. A lovely site, really, once you got home and didn't need to worry about getting around through ever-more increasingly im-passable streets. Few kids, if any, bothered going door-to-door for Halloween that year.

The snow piled up inch after inch as the sun went down… and it fell all night… and was well over 24-inches deep by morning. Looking out from my apartment window in St. Paul, the parking lot below me was a sea of deep white waves, with drifts over five feet high covering garage doors, and all the cars buried window-high with freshly fallen snow.

The buses weren't moving and police advised against any unneces-sary travel, so most people decided to not even try getting to work that day. Good advice, since there was no realistic way of getting one's car out of the lot, and the streets had not been plowed. So

I stayed home, too… and enjoyed watching more and more snow fall all morning, even as the sky turned blue and sunny by noon.

Well, by afternoon, some folks just had to get moving – had to dig their cars out of the snowdrifts… out into the still unplowed parking lot… and get them to the city street, which was at least 100 feet away… and hope to have enough clearance and power to slosh through unplowed streets, now deeply furrowed by some brave (and crazy) drivers who had trucks or SUVs large enough to clear the dense snow.

Looking down out my window I saw that one young woman, maybe 25 or so, had corralled some friends or bystanders to help dig out her car from a giant snowbank. After much work, they finally got the car heading in the right direction toward the street… but there was simply too much deep snow in the parking lot that stymied forward progress.

These guys even hooked up a chain from the back bumper of their SUV to the front bumper of her car and tried to pull her car forward… one guy in the SUV, she in her car, and about three guys pushing on the back of her car… push… push… push… but all to no avail.

After 10 minutes of building frustration, in a last ditch effort to get the car moving, the group huddled one last time, with lots of talk and pointing fingers and waving arms and such, and the woman kind of nodding her head and probably thinking she could still make it to her afternoon shift that day, and only an hour late.

I guess they thought that if they put a little slack in the chain, they could "snap" the car out of its ruts – the way a water skier on one ski is snapped out of shallow water by leaving a little slack in the tow rope – and the forward momentum would carry the SUV and the car safely to the street.

File that thought under, "It Seemed Like a Good Idea at the Time." Or maybe just, "Dumb Ideas."

Still watching from my window, I just thought, "uh oh, don't do it."

With about 9 or 10 feet of slack in the chain, one guy in the SUV, she in her car and three guys waiting to push… the guy in the SUV hit the gas. And even though his wheels were spinning a bit, the vehicle surged forward rather impressively – and proceeded to pull the front grill, the radiator, the lights and the bumper off the front of the car, and drag the whole shooting match about 30 feet down the way before it all came to a rest.

Within seconds, the woman bolted out from her car and ran toward the grill of her car, wrapped in chains, lying haplessly in the snowy parking lot and, stunned, sort of froze while hovering over it, silent, not sure what had just happened, nor what she was looking at.

It must have been sort of an out-of-body experience for her, though no one was hurt, seeing her beloved car torn asunder by friends. I felt sorry for her later, but was laughing so hard by then it was hard to remember exactly what happened next.

Without a radiator and lights, I don't think the woman made it to work that day. I'm not sure what happened to the woman or her friends, but later that day I saw that the car had been pushed back into a parking spot. It disappeared in a few days.

If there's a moral to the story, it's that you just can't fight Mother Nature. It also helps to have friends who are not knuckleheads.

Jeff S., St. Paul, MN

LAWS OF THE UNIVERSE

There are certain things ordained by the heavens to happen. Below is just a small collection of a few of these that I have observed.

Whenever you have an arm load of groceries, tools, kids, you name it, and go for your keys to unlock a door, they will be in the pocket on the same side as the load you're carrying.

Whenever you go shopping with your wife and stand next to what you think is an out-of-the-way rack of clothing, that will be the rack all of the ladies want to look at.

Whenever you have a favorite food at a particular restaurant and look forward all week to getting there for a meal, that's when a) the restaurant goes out of business, or b) your favorite item has been dropped from the menu.

The number of red lights you will hit is inversely proportional to the time you have to get where you're going; that is, with a lot of time, you will encounter few lights, with less time you will hit every f*#@ing one of them.

The tallest people always head to the front of the theater, concert hall, classroom…and generally sit in front of me. Ditto for fat people sitting next to me on an airplane.

Author

BATTING PRACTICE

1964 was a scary time—cold war, spies, and intrigue. As teens, my boyfriend and I were certainly not immune to the fervor. I had been an exchange student in Mexico the summer of '63, so in return, the son, Robertito, came to stay with our family, outside of Philadelphia. He was a defiant, 14-year-old, but a church-going Catholic. At a local Spanish-language church, he'd met and been actively befriended by a Cuban priest. As luck would have it, the FBI had the priest under surveillance and believed him to be a full-fledged spy. They had shared their suspicion with my parents. Being naïve and somewhat shocked, our family just went on with our daily lives. One night at about 3 AM, my boyfriend and I had snuck back to the family room in complete violation of the house rules when the phone rang. Startled, without thinking, Jack quickly answered: "there's a bomb in the mailbox," a gruff, accented voice mumbled. Wavering only a second, Jack grabbed a tiny, plastic, blue baseball bat, and went out swinging. He found himself standing helplessly in the driveway, bat in hand to attack the bomb, as the lights went on in parents' bedroom. No bomb, no heroism, just a lot of explaining required. Robertito left a few days later, and Jack, my protector, became the one under surveillance—of the parental variety.

Deborah S., Huntington Beach, CA

THOSE NO-TOUCH YEARS

AAH, a daughter's love for her father...there's nothing like it. Unless it's in those years when no touching is allowed!

Author

NO GOOD DOGS

Several years ago, a friend of mine, who was always called "Bud" by his parents, was driving his grandmother to his parent's house for dinner. She was a small, frail woman. Upon arrival, he helped her from the car, and walked up the driveway to the house. At that point, his parents' large and rambunctious Black Lab came bounding out of the house, rushed up to grandma, and greeted her by putting its paws on her shoulders. Bud was prepared for this, and had a firm grip on her.

After they subdued the dog, grandma turned to Bud and said "Bud, it seems like all the good dogs are dead."

Dave B. St. Paul, MN

DEAR MR. BUS DRIVER

One of the boys on my elementary route was a tall and stocky kid named Eric. Although he was generally a nice kid, who I liked, he was inclined to shove other kids around. One day as the bus was loading at the end of the school day, he beat up a much smaller kid on the bus. I grabbed him and told him that until I received a note from his parents, he would not be able to ride the bus anymore.

After a week or so without any sign of Eric, he walked up the steps of the bus and handed me a note. Written in a child's scrawl was the following: "Dear Mr. Bus Dirver [sic]. Eric has my permission to ride the bus again. Sincerely, Erics [sic] Mom."

I read the note, struggling to keep a straight face, and said "OK Eric. As long as you brought this note from your mom, you can ride the bus again, but don't ever fight again on this bus." It was an obvious forgery, but I was impressed by his audacity, and wanted him to feel that he really put one over on me. It has occurred to me that my response to his note may have galvanized him to pursue a life of deception. He may have become one of those fellows we read about these days who constructs Ponzi Schemes and ends up in prison.

Dave B., St. Paul, MN

AUTHOR BIO

Gary Oberts is not someone you would invite to a party to light up a room. In fact, at a party you will most often find him in a corner just watching people and taking mental notes on how funny they can be.

Gary grew up in Rockford Illinois in a typical suburban, middle class setting. He attended Catholic school through 10th grade and therein obtained a tremendous amount of material for books like this. He then went on to college at Northern Illinois University and majored in geology. College life during the late 1960s-early 1970s was a real trip, which is why he doesn't remember much of it and hence has essentially nothing from those years in this book. He did, however, work in a paint factory during those years to support his learning habit. Those factory years provided him with a wealth of material, some of which you will see here, maybe some a little later.

In 1971 Gary met the love of his life, Kristin, whom he married in a little over a year. Their life together has generated many laughable moments, but those of you who are married know that discretion is the lifeblood of marriage, so again, you won't find many stories about the married life here…yet.

After college, Gary and Kristin moved to Connecticut and then on to Wisconsin for both work and college. Eventually, they settled in Minnesota where Gary continued his career in water resources (hydrology) and Kristin in information management.

They raised two kids (lots of stories you will see them) and spent about 35 years in the tundra.

Coming to their senses in 2008, they took early retirements and moved to Tustin California where they have lived happily ever after.